Positive Pea

To mum and dad for always supporting me.

Published in association with Bear With Us Productions

Illustration by Marcel Trindade
Graphic design by Katie Owens

www.justbearwithus.com

Positive Pea

Every child should grow up
feeling happy, in a happy world.
Be like Positive Pea.

In a big green field on a big green farm,
With a smile every day, always quiet and calm,
Near his many great friends who he loved to see,
Lived a happy little fellow called Positive Pea.

Pea was full of joy, full of love and cheer,
He always found happiness would overcome fear,
He loved every weather – spring, summer or fall,
And he loved other veggies – he was friends with them all!

But some veggies living on the big green farm,
Weren't positive at all, and they lacked Pea's charm.
There were unhappy veggies of all different kinds,
And Pea had a mission ..to change their minds.

There was Sad Broccoli, who was always upset,
Come rain or shine, he'd be crying, you bet.
He didn't like silence and he didn't like noise.
He was too shy to play and he didn't like toys.

And then Angry Carrot, who never ever smiled,
Any little nuisance made her temper go wild.
The grumpiest veg that you ever would meet,
Always red with anger, she looked like a beet!

But Pea would help with their sadness and fear,
He would give them a smile, and lend them an ear.
All around the farm as he strolled along,
His happy little voice sung a happy little song..

"Good morning bees!
Good morning trees!
Good morning everyone, from Positive Pea!
I feel so free,
And full of glee,
Let's all be as happy as me!"

"Good Morning Sad Broccoli!" Pea said that day,
But Broccoli was too sad to know what to say,

"It's okay if you feel full of sorrow and dread,
Smile, the world will seem brighter ahead!"

"Good Morning Angry Carrot!" said Positive Pea,

"I wish you wouldn't smile and be happy near me.
What's good about morning? It's the worst time of day.
Scram, Pea, go and find somewhere else to play."

"Leave us alone, you strange little thing,
We are simple veggies, we don't laugh, play or sing.

We aren't always daft and silly like you,
You're making us feel worse! Now go on, Pea, shoo!"

“Oh Broccoli, Carrot, there’s no need to be grumps!
No need to sit there like sad, angry lumps!
The field we live in is better with a friend,
Together we can take on the world, in the end!“

Broccoli sighed, saying "Pea, you're so small!
How is it you're afraid of nothing at all?"

"Your size doesn't matter! If you THINK big and bold,
You can do ANYTHING. You can win gold!"

"No!" Carrot said, "Those are just distractions!
You need to stay put, be careful of your actions!
Stay where you are! Stand still and grow!"

"Why grow up without hap-pea-ness, though?"

Broccoli wanted to turn his mood around!
"What is happiness, though?" he asked, with a frown.

"Hap-pea-ness is sunshine, hap-pea-ness is rain,
And it's every day, when I see your face again!"

"Happiness is hard" said Carrot, all annoyed,
"With tractors, and people, and pests to avoid,

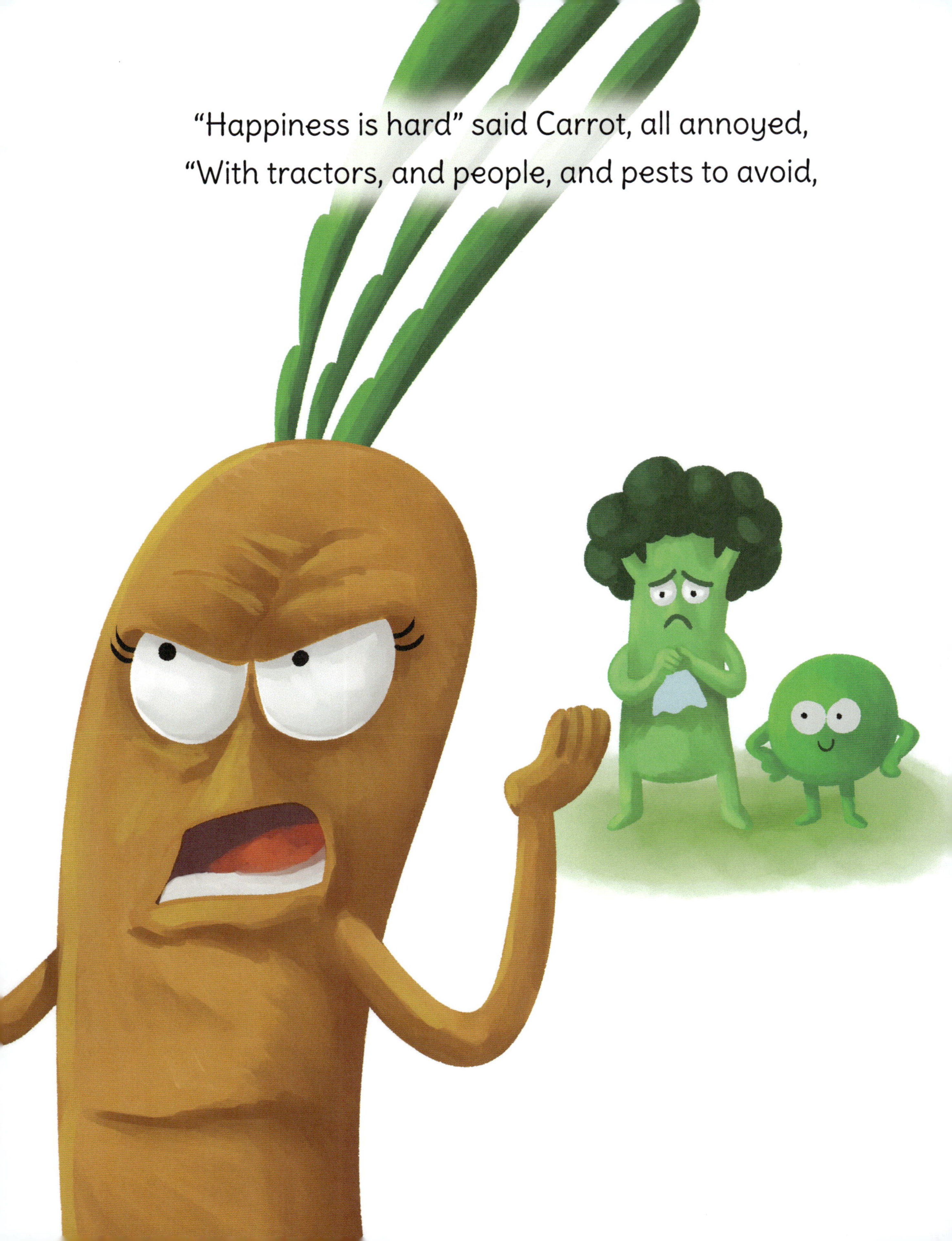

We might end up being eaten by that mole."

"I only popped up to say hallo! I'll go back in my hole!"

“The tractor is scary, but it’s just a machine!
It’s big and loud, but it keeps the farm clean!
Positivity’s not about pretending,
It’s seeing the good – in every little thing!”

"Happiness is hard, Carrot, very true!
No one's happy every single day, through and through.
It's OK to have bad days that feel sad and long,
Sometimes things feel difficult and wrong."

"I was a single Pea, all on my tod,
But now we're together, three peas in a pod!
We all have a purpose, we all have a mission,
Together we're amazing! The best edition!"

As night drew near, they thought for a while,
Broccoli smirked and Carrot gave a smile.
Broccoli said "Right! I won't get sad or cry!"
Carrot said "Right! I'll give cheerfulness a try!"

So Carrot, Broccoli and Positive Pea,
Watched the sun set as a company.

Even Sad Broccoli cracked a big smile!

Even Angry Carrot felt calm for a while!

“These problems are solvable it seems to me,
With work they can be lovable!” Said Broccoli.

“Its okay to not be okay! So long as you try!
Everything can get better!” Came Pea’s reply.

Carrot looked at Pea feeling quiet and glad,
"I promise I won't get impatient or mad!"

And Broccoli said with a big green grin,
"I'll always know how to let happiness in!"

"Sleep well, friends," said Positive Pea,
"Tomorrow will be a great day – you'll see!
Cool, Calm Carrot, you'll be Cosy, first Class!
Brave Bright Broccoli, as Bold as Brass!"

And you'll be best friends with little old me:
A Prim, Proud, Playful, Positive Pea!

The End

STAY POSITIVE!

Printed in Great Britain
by Amazon

63017603R00022

If you focus on the wonderful things around you such as nature and friends, you can learn to have a more happy out-look, just like Positive Pea.

BEAR WITH US PRODUCTIONS

www.justbearwithus.com

ISBN 978-1-5272-9666-4

9 781527 296664